SOUND ARCHIVE

i Mam Bont a Myles

NERYS WILLIAMS
SOUND ARCHIVE

SEREN

Seren is the book imprint of
Poetry Wales Press Ltd.
57 Nolton Street, Bridgend, Wales, CF31 3AE
www.serenbooks.com

The right of Nerys Williams to be identified as
the author of this work has been asserted in accordance
with the Copyright, Designs and Patents Act, 1988.

ISBN: 978-1-85411-538-6

A CIP record for this title is available from the British Library.

The publisher acknowledges the financial assistance of
the Welsh Books Council.

Cover art: Aine Venables 'Bird Type' 2010, mixed media.

Printed in Bembo by The Berforts Group Ltd, Stevenage

Author's website: http://melopoeia.blogspot.com

Contents

Kinetic Melodies

It is easy to speak of language as ownership,
your purring phonemes are not my right
nor any dialogic imagination.

It is like the time I mixed metaphors
and found myself nude, addressing a crowd
with no immediate

parallel or paradox to flail at.
An empty lectern, a thousand eyes.

Small inconsistencies alert us:
a time to find a colour of saying,
how dialect forms the melody of tall tales.

After storm fields have disappeared
sulphur fills the air where the tree stands.

Here it says *I am branch*
root and hollow, rub my charcoal into clean hands,
serenade me with your speech,
curse the carrion crow below.

The Dancing House

for Josef Capek

In the perfect future of the past
there is a glass book on the sideboard.

The dead converse
with the angel at your shoulder
who finds time to stroke your hair.

There was a heart punched in the ticket
the heart became a diamond
to engrave a heart of stone.

With eyes of frozen cobalt
the angel says:

After the forced flight – dark.
After the spinning dial – water.
After the telling – echo.

We are searching *The Dancing House* –
the angel and I.

He tells me of sound wave terrorists at sea
breaking the whale's song
distressing the dolphins
changing their acapella to frenzy.
Or, the story of oceans as our nostalgia.

The cockatoo sings a lazy samba
eye frozen to emerald.
Again and again he croons:

there will always be spring
there will always be a curator.

I came here looking for the child's drawing
in a hall of a thousand drawings.

I came searching for the perfect title:
Flowers, Clogs, How All of Us Outgrew Our Shoes.

I am not a sociable person – I do not think so.
I am not a brave person – I do not think so.
If I could write on a butterfly's wing would I succeed?
I could fill the drawers with your anecdotes.

The bird blushes to brighten his wings.
Beware of dictionaries falling from the sky.
Beware of hijacked mothers, persistent fathers
and letters in reverse.

Bring your love in a paper bag and leave it on the mantle.
Beware of telling the turning tide to sing
since whoever lies is not believed
even when speaking the truth.

I came here to find a child's picture.
I came here to tango around the paint points.
I came here to slow dance with history.

All this really happened once –
Believe me says the frozen angel
with a ruby eye, seeking salutations
in the corridors of *The Dancing House.*

Escher's Lens

1

Enter the blue room – a pair of child's clogs on a wall.
Enter the red room – a pair of worn mules.
Enter the green room – find the glass slipper.

Late last night a voice told me, *you choose*
a stack of pictures, *choose your survivor.*

The close-cropped hair, walking sticks,
eyes of children, you choose.
You choose, the saliva on lip,
the missed thread from a new shirt.

2

It is where three contours meet:
the holding of the inventory
the gesture from hand to figure.

An affection of fist clenching pencil
to march into still life.

The circuitry of a village.
Cars speeded to chase zero.
How cats find gravity in movement.
How the centre of a butterfly's wing
spirals in circumvention.

Yes, I too saw the admiral fly across the lens,
an orange magnified in circuitry,
bedouin tent in thought's pendulum.

But nothing –
Nothing, prepared me
for the incline of your neck.

3

The man with the starfish sonata in his head tells me:
There are three points to your turning:

Take care with the dark, keep beat with brevity
and never waste time.

Those were barnacles that were his eyes.
I am he says *writing* The Book of Aphorisms,

erasing The Book of Aphorisms *with boot polish and a blowtorch.*
It makes a poor living but such is life.

His arms open and from his chest
bursts a magenta bird, a neon sign

and a turquoise tiger. *I am sent to sing, portion*
and patrol the word in magic. He asks:

Do you believe in rhetoric without syntax?
Do you believe in Bendigeidfran and Pwyll?

Do you believe in blindness and insight?
Do you believe in a mother's smile?

Do you believe in a language of the gods?
Do you believe in intoxication?

Do you believe in repression?
Do you consider barbarity?

Do you believe in experimentation?
Do you believe in telling the truth?

Conversations with Cocteau

Villefranche-sur-Mer

1

You tell me the worst thing for a poet
is to be admired through being misunderstood.

And in your call to order I see you
fashion the *Potomak*, your aquarium creature,

taunting the poet-albatross wearing your skin-tight,
adjective-tight leather trousers.

Your matador cape, a comet's tail
chasing Picasso through the glyphs
of a cubed village near the sea.

2

Entering your mural is not difficult,
easier on the eye than poetry's religion with no hope.

Arc into clef into key
the sea-salt world in parabola.

I have seen sea horses dancing
and breath blow sand across ocean floors.

At the surface is a man walking on water
shoulders held by invisible strings.

Peter worried at such strangeness
unaware that angels work at reef knots.

Harness to guide his *splish splosh*
waking bloaters, sting rays and seals.

He walks the circumference of the chapel's spine
to the last corner and the cock's crow.

3

Always there is beauty to lead the becoming,
not that we have lost our vocabulary.

Arms in a passage remain holding candelabras,
tender thoughts on human pain.

Orphée, the beast and me-ridiculous walk to the quay
gold-shoed on this feast night for a wedding.

Our faces echo morphemes of doubt,
while the moon-rabbit pounds rice for his supper.

The Convalescent

*Rule 1. The drawing is the discord. Rule 2. The atmosphere is the
notes seen at a distance. Paint the atmosphere & its complementary.*
(Gwen John: *Notebooks*)

Ten times over, sketched in variation coloured by construction,
bistre, combage, blues, lacs, mole, caput mortuum.

A young woman sometimes reading a letter,
a book, rose-teapot, glass, a plate by her side.

Interior, still ill skin clinging to a blue dress,
designing a life in colourwash.

The render is ochre her chair wicker,
light breaks at intervals in the room.

Was it given? Records unsure.
Hands sculpting hard now,

blobbing the chrome down face, brow, top cushion,
mouth measurement from jaw to end of muscle line.

I was going to bring it to the clinic Isabel said it isn't done.
All those little things have taken away my happiness of giving pleasure.

The ten frames run their encryption,
angles shift, the lowering of the chin,

hair swept, hung, then falling loosely forward,
letter held high, low slight slump in the shoulders.

Her hips and torso straight, painful, awkward.
Each revision a restoration of will.

The Dead Zoo, Dublin

for John Peel

1

In the dead zoo we walk an afternoon
touching the giraffe with a sutured stomach

and the bull seal with a broken ear.
The gazelles too are thinking

about the jungle kings, sun-kissed and light-bleached
making a performance of their anger.

All hips and grimaces the hyenas
pass silent commentary on our clothes.

And I remember finding the bat in daylight
on the schoolyard wall, its cape and hooks

trembling, broken by the colourwash of light,
it hated being stroked.

We had a bat funeral, a ceremony that summer
which followed other rituals:

wreath laying for road kill, bouquets for robins
and elegies for tame jackdaws.

Strange to find oneself here with these exhibitionists
teasing us that they are alive still.

2

Music is a skin,
notes at the tips of my fingers
fingertips at the edge of my song.

After the elegies and the websites
after the obituaries and the radio stories
after the musicians and magazines
after the bulletins and the brouhaha
there was nothing left but teenage kicks.

3

So I take you to the dead zoo
your own private Gethsemane
to curate the animals into action.

4

I will use your words against mine with mine and on mine,
I will play all your records at the same time

the unreleased singles and demos
causing cacophony on the dance floors.

Rhythm is a bright confusion
I will say that music is homesickness

And you can give me your *unheimlich*
as an elegy of recognition.

Sound Archive

for Cliff Anderson

It takes patience this piecing
of noise in an archive for voices.

Chronicled on my silver-silicon
a focus of gravity gone, scene unset.

Tempos in the unthreading
of flight beating.

Misremembered movement
the voice still says:

Do not package me
as an afterthought or a bulletin.

Though I have never been to Spain
I understand attachment theory
and have been told of thanatology.

Raise your glass to this last flourish
as I switch from Andante to Largo

I toast Dubrovnik, Elvis and Chopin
free the slaves of my imagination.

I will wear boaters in the rain
and fill one room with flowers.

I will raise hell in remaining chapels
never searching for injunctions nor pardons.

I will be the sage on the hill
filling in for memorial towers.

I will finish that string quartet
begun at twenty-five.

I will flirt with the ladies at the till
and get my groceries for free.

I will smoke over the baby grand
turning to my right for a tumbler of gin.

I will mark a map of all colours felt
frame them into a continent.

There will be methods to my madness
which I will name kinetic imbalance.

On this day
thought is blown over the wall
over trees to the road,

jazzed up and jiving
a bouquet of spectral dandelions
for you to hold.

Aurascope

You came with Mr Rhetoric
and the light found a pattern
for his squat figure guarding the door.

We sped, or rather I, through countries
I never really knew
while a fire fell in the grate.

The phantom caller sketched my hand
watching the butterfly ring
beat metal spirals on my finger.

My favourite perfume was a room of laughter,
in the sound between my aurascope
clouds emptied of your face.

Shopkeeper's Ledger

for Gwyneth Williams

1

In ice morning we make tramp's tea:
six months from strawberries in hedges
six months from Friesians heavy in fields
six months from not speaking to neighbours.

There is heat rising from fog
and sugar-pop anecdotal evidence on my tongue.

I will speed-dial your singing to the world
through every call centre.

Why is your number not in the directory?
Have you changed your song by deed poll?

2

Your portrait at the counter
sun shifts marks gesture,
how light smiles in points.

Always make up before sleep
and how sleep now makes you.

There was a man chasing me
over the valley and far away
where boiled sweets litter branches
and Candy Rock Mountain *cuts* Marshmallow Hill.

3

The bard tells me poets are androgynous,
sun falls at their shoulders,
grief and colours are felt through skin.
He tells of socialists, co-ops and atomic warfare.
I taste tobacco tar and beer on his tongue.

4

Here is biography in a wooden chest
move it to a lit place for words.

Shopkeeper, granddaughter, diplomat and daughter
to a woman whose soprano died in a goitre.

Shop ledger inheritor I am bound to your bills:
cobbler's nails, sugar, wheat and flour,
lozenges, castor oil and tapioca.

Shackled to a hundred correspondence courses:
How to Make-Believe Mathematics, The Magician's Complaint,

The Followers of Freedom, Finding Time to be Myself,
Watching the World from a Distance, Colouring with Words,

How to Sing across a Valley, Making Humour a Strategy,
The Silver School of Easy Charm and *Serenity of the Smile.*

I am searching the *Encyclopaedia Mythica*
under Niobe and Artemis and Cybele.
Here mountains are carved in a female form
and wrath a scree in their side.

I am searching for a skein of silk
to bind up figures from books.
Your handwriting a measured net
marshalling falling stock.

I am searching for the giggle —
that bubble in your throat.
Or buttons stored in bottles
and fuses in a boot polish tin.

I am searching for the broken lock
to an empty barn in a long field,
where a mirror opens to show
the cleanest emporium in the sky.

The tremolo of the blackbird
bursts through the blue —

the space made finishes.

Shopkeeper's Song

You thought to give me voice
spinning me into your cycle.

You thought that in this singing
gesture could be caught

an eyelid's crease, a finger's folding
a laugh into air above.

There is history in a broken sentence
you are no ventriloquist.

I sang to greet ravens above this village
washing, brushing and mopping

work songs to the world
making sense of soothsayers:

Blessed is the man with a wooden leg
for his wife has only one stocking to mend.

Set the teacups and saucers
on the bench for high tea.

Patterns of bright confusion.
I will say love is homesickness.

How to sing the texture of hair
drying near fire on a winter's night?

Free your stories into air.
Go tell it to the crows.

Jezebel

after T.H. Parry-Williams

Her face gave marble colour
the flashing phalanx of her eyes
held thunder in its making.

The ligaments of her violence
made sound a stream of bullets
beating an iron scree.

I have come to murder the discursive
to stone the innocent
in a time of unholy rule.

By the statues of Baal
and the gardens of Naboth
I swear to my undoing.

Her body thrown to dogs
staining the hooves of king's troops
beyond the wall, bludgeoned meat.

No mausoleum of indifference houses me.
My history finds a form for story
in bloodied rags and screams.

But there are remembrances:
my black hive of hair, the movement of silk
and men with speeches of hunger
watching a gated town.

Marilyn's Auction House

Queuing for relics
diamante dust on typography.

Like the sun-danced lover we search
telling of kisses and filmic cartography.

I study the broach on your lip
how we hug those words:

In vitro injection.

There are gestures found in this jumble
a stray silk, a cracked bead.

Taking inventory of a life
biography in a brochure.

As useful as a stub of lipstick
you touch her jeans, the Misfit ones.

Lassoed three times in combat
stitched into that dress before singing.

In coloured vials a small pin,
a hair slide to bid for.

Refracted dresses of polyester
patterns cupping her breasts.

She breathed desire
into monochrome, acid white, lips pursed.

You touch my hand
as though palms are a sign of indecency.

Loie Fuller's Dancing School

I am terpsichorean
a figure in burlesque.

Sometimes Miss Pepper stranded on the prairie
sometimes Buffalo Bill's navvy
sometimes a soubrette.

Imagine my surprise at the spectacular
a bijou opera house.

An alien in melodrama
Aladdin-girl in melos.

In the cave of the fire of life,
I am Ayesha of two thousand years

finding a silhouette
within slimness.

Such methods of the divine
becomes a gal from Chicago.

Methane Sonata

The Titan moons of Mars hold repetitions.
There is ice that is not ice
sky rains methane in shards
tough as platinum bullets.

At a juncture in the sky
gods console one another

a plain that becomes
the anteroom of the dark.

The story of how a hard head
makes for a warm heart.

★

As we watched the falling debris
crystalline, my father

tells of his grandfather returning dead drunk.
Grandmother banishing him to bed

finds him at morning an umbrella over his head:
Waiting for the storm the line that never falters
a pantomime in symmetry, Mrs Hale-Bop.

★

The child wants a dandelion set in glass.
The mother a book on eschatology.
The minister is happy with a stuffed owl
his own sagacious theology.

Somewhere Mr Pierrot whispers:
There is a broken mirror far away
without the mouthing gaze
and arms that hold you tight.

I mean your biography
not your bibliography.

With smudged eyeliner
and silk pantaloons
Mr Pierrot is nobody's buffoon
his ringtone is dire samba.

★

Listen to our satellite songs
monitors of dark matter:
spy cameras for *Life Channel Inc.*
and *Plagiarism.com.*

Space hardware sonatas
master this acid lightshow
in a pattern of flight.

A flash at the size of Africa
a rendition of Puerto Rico.
Tin cans in equivalence
my fierce Tinkerbells

hosts to the Caliban beneath.

Global Warriors

In squat fields we create our homes
overnight hay houses, historic.

Crawling through entries, musing at windows
we are wanderers, betrayers.

All day we wait for
fire-eaters, night predators.

We travel nightly.
Leaving a trail is not difficult.
Oxen pull us towards the next sun.

Water rots. Colour shifts. When grey blight
and mildew blossom we need return.

The chill draws us to stone, crystal, pyrites
landlocked we listen in our cave's echo –

waiting for sheeted ice, for smoke,
waiting for heat to ambush.

Penguin Love

A strike on air with a visor's cast
stationed shoe-gazing others siphoning mist

a community of sextants, angled at constellations,
limpets on a road of fish skulls.

Jostling for conversation, their answer
a tight wire hammered at intervals.

Full of the disappointments
of fairy tales, the grey ones quiver waiting

for the first breach of yellow and puff-balled chests.
Or, the story of making smooth.

The Book of Aphorisms

1

In finding you wanting
I waited for the letter to arrive

the bleached lithograph
with ten times ten-eyed monsters in green
the sea-lipped serif.

You told me that pornography
lacked imagination – its mouth
a violation of future thought.

Instead you taught me the pornography of the sea.
As I chased the syllables
of your broken angel through corridors of pine
past meadowsweet, into dunes too tall to fight in.

We found your favourite aphorism
the phrasing of nation.

Three tellings of the triad
the triptych of a tale:
sound, sequence, and *event.*

The sounding of power is a hollow
braying in disordered light,
a cacophony of ill crows.

While the sequence
arranges mythmaking.

A strata of rocks
burying a plain of words.

The event is what we continue
to await

something will happen
just out of reach, never healing the *now*.

As if order is no more
than indices in sand, systems of belief
or a corruption of flight.

2

Here I am thinking of the phalanx of your thought
your breath which although measured has no inclusive.

How the dark locks the pupils
how anamnesis cannot be dressed in epithets.

But what happens, when memory has no template to work from?

3

There is a room next to mine
I know him not

but always a tray outside his door
a laugh near my partition wall.

I am scared I scar too easily
each blow finds a tenant on my skin.

I am afraid to seduce lest it place my plan in peril.
Will this day be that?

Though seduction has its guidelines
to mouth uncertainties at a mirror,

I could never beat all the icons,
Byzantium spectators with aureoles of thought.

4

My books bury your books
my sentences smother your sentences.

I know why she sang across the valley
hymns too tall with their tales of night
branding light.

Tell no one
speak of no one.

Her letters in the boot of his car.
What is half an hour between lovers?

What I miss: detergent, mints, paraffin,
banknotes in a broken bag.

In the search for symmetry I file these letters to the imaginary:

There is a tall building. Find the method. Watch your back.
Part on good terms. The supposed child of.

Let me be there. Give me the rain god.
Allegedly owned by.

Say the no name to nobody.

Cypher

after Eurydice

I am folding into myself
my stem cells furling memory

the first beacon of desire
its first breach of power
      – I fold into myself

the second song of delay
the second word's colour
      – I furl into myself

the third salt pillar of loss
a third method in madness
      – I fly into myself

I am description refusing to unscroll
a mauve curlicue in the bruised flower...

pattern without perspective
a circled centre beyond circumference...

ignorance with no shame
an affidavit with no name....

It is a form of therapy
      says the attendant with an unlaced shoe.
Which will create your posterity
      adds the magician without a cape.
Come and seek your destiny
      calls the astrologer with a henna tattoo.

Anecdotes are coming up on the screen:

read them
      write them
            rehearse them to me....

Becoming a blind bulb is not easy.

Since it is neither retreat nor recovery
      monitor the amnesiac in blue-green and magenta.
Since it is neither bright nor dark
      wake the narcoleptic from dream-circuitry.
Since it is neither right nor wrong
      kiss the aphasic with a ribboned tongue.

My unthreading refutes supplication.

      And sight?
      It's a firebrand
      to the smoothness I've become.

Canter's Starstruck Diner, L.A.

All we recall are the stuccos on the wall
and lighting in glass leaves overhead.

We move towards the telescope of tin
the short man nestles under his eye,

he knows the telephone directories
of starlets that passed by

the incandescent blue
to no-hope gin.

My friends have the confidence of
Californian Jays,

police their love of scripts and film
with fire alarms and parking lots.

Our man takes a bow
and tells us how

the epic flew to far-flung sets
and Westwood vignettes.

Everything is coming up Vine and Rose
he cries

All the president's men
will receive while they can

the purple hearts and cellophane seals
of the re-routed wheels.

While my commerce continues
in the dedication of dreams,

I will give you a tablet of stone
to trace a long way home

not Rosetta, it will tell
the weather of signs.

How grenades can be made
to protect those most afraid,

following the brace of
burlapped squirrels to a habitation.

Indeed a human hibernation
without climate change.

The Maestro

After the magpies cats and canaries
      bebop improv and free-form,
      the composers in profile, the manuscript case
      lock broken, sheaves unread.
After the performance and the payment
let no man say there is not humour
a terrible humour in the day's end.
Its gash beginning
of magpies
with cats
and canaries.

Playing host in a white tux
fifty years in the background
of romance and jazzed-up blues.
Training Mac to send in the clowns
allowing Porgy to plead with Bess.

Tell me Maestro is this your manifesto for absolution?
Tell me Maestro is this what you need to hear?

Here it comes again
    it is obsessional
        indicative.
        In counterpoint
   it is pervasive
      a divining dance
      drawn in
that beat up
rhythm
of Chopin's indigo blues.

Listen to the tyrannical
the megalomanical
shaking each porcelain bust
one by one to the floor.

Tracing the arc of your samba
I trail you to the supermarket.

You feed five thousand on economy bread
decanting water into wine.

Freeing swallowtails into the rafters
and watch the joint – jumping.

Wrote to you yesterday and here you come today
       Obsessional
Sang of you yesterday and here you come today
       Compulsive
Baby, you can't love me and treat me this way.

Taking the long journey home
in this fjord you sit on deck

a baby grand ballasted with limpets
sea anemones as your epaulettes.

Breaking the anagram of the soundboard
you steal a riff from Beethoven's third.

Starboard – a string quartet serenades the Leviathan
braving the deep with bad timing.

Ice mountain's breath
makes rivets of your knuckles, marble of your lungs.

Your swaying tells me
this is...
this is...
all too much.

There are details you remember

as memory becomes
the movement of a horse
thrown into lightning, over a gate
tumbling into a tree.

Taking a crotchet, a minim and a quaver
as measure of life lived.

The Pedagogical Poet

1

You say there is always equivalence:
the rainbow and star,
journalist and politician,
mothers and daughters.

I set it as a bridge beyond me,
two hands before the frog
as he jumps into my grasp,
a hurried eye in new warmth.

How, he must wonder, was that done?
The beat to limb meeting hand
sensing blood, touching skin.

You say there is always reason,
molehills which cannot be mountains,
regrets which only service nostalgia.

I take this as time to find pattern:
how the ice leaf holds form,
how degrees of separation
require more empathy during war.

Figures on facsimile remind me of you.
Footnotes on the document resound into the blue.

2

I took my pedagogical poet to sea
dressed him in robes
fitting of such high incidents
of narrative serendipity.

I brushed his hair
and painted his skin with calligraphy,
medieval memories
salt and love inscribed with glyphs.

I slit his tongue to a fork
so he could breathe more easily,
hiss at his enemies
spit and curse explicitly.

But the sea was unkind
and laughed at his knees.

3

The pedagogical poet invested in immortality.
He found a broker who bargained
in free versification.

When asked his ambition
he replied *pebbles in my mouth,*
a white studio cube.

I need a payment for a ton of clay,
I will build a beehive
around my body.

Marked in iambs
my house, the dolmen of dreams
will create a Celtic dawn.

The pedagogical poet added elliptically,
where there is mastery there is little mystery.

I was found in a time capsule
with a robin's egg, sextant,
seismograph, a volume of parodic poetry,
a map of furthest places, a bakelite ashtray
and an overcoat from Bon Marché.

I did not acquire language easily,
but sang to my keepers
(an aged man and woman who farmed bees).
My singing caused scandal – my French Provençal.

National exhibit number one:
a man who attracts moths and martyrs
rondas, vespers, sonatas, symphonies cascade from his mouth.

The virtuoso musicophiliac, next to the monster with no-name,
the girl with no lips and the mother of the moon.

Trust me I give you rhythm
trust me I am a millionaire poet
trust me I am the dark star on the moon.

Don't you understand the wherefore of thou?
Don't you understand The Three Trolls in the Forest?
What of The Princess and the Pea?

In *The Happy House of Rings*
our relationship reached its crisis.

Cursing at the firebrand of jewellery
my pedagogical poet swore at idolatry,

tore out all anthologies of wedding poetry,
their lacklustre combinations of philology

and what he called *versifications in depravity*,
he drew up the trapdoor and fell into the Liffey.

Even now the tabloids tell of a pallid man
a face of oxide with mulberry lipstick,

waving at albatrosses, canvassing
a people's poetry library.

But between you and me,
he left to conjugate the sound of sea.

An Anatomy of Arguments

1

Trespass rests on a form yet unknown
that is to say a word inserted here
could alter the licence of relation.

Edges so fine their chords fray into light,
all the rehearsed attacks:
wisdom pieces, fire commas.

Takes a genius to know it for what it is,
a person of myth, carrying a
talisman of spun nettles,

weaving the ragged hole until it rests
on a pattern you know must soon
if not now, assert itself.

2

Always lustre in the call from eye to lip,
as we sign one another in caution.

Could I call it tenacity?
The light moving sure now,

there it flickers in a smile
and the hand shapes the jaw.

Motes between us – the face we see
knowing paper whisperers.

3

When I break this space, it is neither reserve nor policy
for worry of what happens, each atom drained.

When we finally speak of our features
there will be sudden strangeness.

Taking in each profile separately,
a numerical sight. No airless room to lock,
an archive of signs.

4

The woman stealing flowers by the bus queue
greets another with a flurry of carnations.

Bewilderment and unaffected recognition:
happiness I am beloved by a stranger on the street.

Until the shopkeeper snatches back her own.
Laughed? If only there was more time.

5

A tenancy of words where properties
of inaction take equal defence.

Meanwhile, the agent in her coat and shades
radios the alphabet cosmos:

It is time to make amends
Let's write it up in halogen this time.
Take it from here: BE AWARE.
WATCH THE SKIES. KEEP ON LOOKING.

Dolls

after Takeshi Kitano

Even when I tell you I've lost all sense of my feet:
the arch that made those prints – broken
the stem that was my spine – faulty.
    Still you come with ribbons
    to lace invisible shoes
    a susurrus over my blank body.

This is a cord between wandering beggars
its silk as sound as the dye that made it strong,
a red ribbon whose tug tells of retreat,
    its shackle a memory regret
    the signature of a legislator.

Argus-eyed you wait for gods
mistaking their appointments.
The operator gives you a song
to connect cloud and blossom,
fire-wind and ice-storm,
while seas burn a note of beginning.

Beesting

I found your money tree
a broken cello followed,
No 10 – it is the *Harp*.

You always knew a good tune
quartets for cold weather,
colour of ice.

The book of days
the buckle for your shoe
the saxophone on your watch.

Stalked by the preacher man
the voyeur that time forgot,
linguistic menace.

Seal Pharaoh's eyes with beeswax –
build a temple to the sound
of misheard melody.

The book of days
the buckle for your shoe
the saxophone on your watch.

Our service of laughter
clandestine me,
we smoke at air.

Breaking the jitterbug
matriculate desire,
its community of songs.

I came to your door
for the metronome,
pacing stories with memory.

The book of days
the buckle for your shoe
the saxophone on your watch.

How to Make Things Disappear

1

The small dog brushed against
the paisley print of childhood

a snagged ball in the mouth
of a wagging creature.

How to prise recollection
from poetry at war.

To suture a gloved hand
in the symmetry of a blue jay's wing.

It was never my intention
to make suffering a sign.

Although they stopped using verdigris
in the nineteenth century

green is still a holy colour.
See Muhammed's coat –
important men are given a green halo.

2

Mr Spider where are you going to be
when the dark tries to see me?

Mr Spider what are you going to do
when the morning don't carry me through?

Mr Spider who will you kiss
when light makes its draft of this?

Mr Spider where are you going to be
when the light sees too much of me?

Mr Spider can it be twice true
that friend I made a fool of you?

3

SHUT UP shouts the musician at the crowd
LISTEN BEFORE IT IS LOST.

I am sorry it is years since I performed in public.

My mouth is dry, my frame awkward,
I am not used to talking.
My words are ribbons in a box,
mismatched buttons in bag.

VANISH has replaced POLISH,
MAGIC has become EXPLOSION,
BREVE is a synonym for BREATH,
MONSTROUS battles with MONOPOLY.

4

My owl flies at five
face hidden from the world.

His wings taut brown
to the faraway tree
at the edge of the field.

He searches sudden movement
to guide his passage.

Last Night a Radioman Saved My Life

for Myles

I found the Emerald Tablet
the Alchemist's rod
walked the seven miles to your house
in bad weather.

You sat in a circle of judo players
a figure in clown's trousers
and no make up.

The ju-ju man
the bwci bo
broadcaster
in wardrobes
you are not.

At the call of the conductor
they found the censored papers,
ledgers of time and breathing rights
in papier maché globes.
They burnt your archive of signs.

The ju-ju man, bwci bo broadcaster that you are not.

In the permafrost there is a box marked echopraxia.
In the permafrost there is a box marked palipraxia.
In the permafrost there is a box marked hydra with
    a thousand heads.

Memory advances repetition through desire.
My heart has taken its own illogical end
to a framed conclusion.
For I have seen kryptonite in those hills
and an alphabet on fire.

It may be easier to outlive the end of the universe
in a dance of abandon

with Moses of Osmosis, Judas of Judo
and a Magdalene mother.

But I prefer the interference on the set,
its white noise quintet
deciphering the unreadable.

My ju-ju man, bwci bo broadcaster that you are not.

Graveyard Mural Man

All surfaces must beam, you whispered,
the web, the finger-trail, the mineral grain.

Unveiling your masterpiece –
patterns of stone tattoos,
cracked logarithms and heat.

I forgot that these are stones for burying.
The near sun with fronds arched

dancing above the tune of a psalm
with a cloak and crown
as though life depended upon it.

Scraping the lichen into curlicues,
this sullen man exhibits his taste
for memorializing with silver paint.

He must have thought that now was time
to fill these names in.

Caldy

for Jonathan

The boy with visions of cherubs and sated sight
finds relief in these corridors.
Three hours I walk with him

through canyons, the brilliance of glass,
swords and unearthed relics,
he builds sepulchres with his hands.

Effigies and talismans swoon at his touch,
he finds impediments to knowledge
in a catacomb of scribes.

I am the sign, a cicatrix on a mother's breast
a serif in the sand, the torturer's sweat
the colour of the clan, an angel's breath.

Slackened to a bow, the sage kneels
laughing at whispers, bright-eyed
with the calyx of a question:

Do you know your true love? He will speak
his name patterned in a cone of flowers,
the call of a cracked bell, a view of cloudy stars.

Trust this since my trust in you is now complete.

Hello Again, It's Me

for Dai Rhyd-Fawr

The gap in exclamation could be
fire turning in my hands,
as one by one tangerines fall

They die. Black-robed we dance the corridor
mortar board over your eyes
the tassel skims, so we tread carefully.

Anecdotal me –
an earphone each, it is hymn night again.
She finds her past and cries.

Her dress is cheap, cardigan too small,
voice too big for her mouth.
We furl the words back.

She speaks of steel, galvanized cans
smelting and Sunday school.
Singing does not help.

Fear of the fall,
a crack seen in floorboards.
What do you see?

Same quiet before struggle,
symmetry in expression.

Glâs to glass: blue to bottled,
your clauses fray instinctively.

Hammering on phrases not on doors,
self-made description pummelled in.

Bathing Beauty

Late afternoon the women would ask
for the timetable of the bath.

Comfort of lather, hoisting of skirts
peeling to sudden nakedness,
mirror to steam.

Heparin bodies, maps of history
playground tattoos,
scars of childbirth.

Bubbles forming half-hid words
rocks in throat,
stories in threads.

Sleep comes easier after heat and moisture
after talk of fragrance, talc and fashion
after righting the body.

All my mimeographed mothers
entering enveloped beds.

My Singing Zookeeper

I am here you are gone there are birds there will be song.

An owl in the chimney at morning.
An owl in the chimney at half-light.

I saw it, I saw it, a big owl, a brown owl,
it made a pretty picture.

Bigger than my book of birds, bigger than this book in leather,
a bound book, a trophy.

A trophy I made, a trophy I made in London Zoo.
An elephant brain, the kingdom's biggest brain.

I worked it, I worked it, I worked it clean.
The biggest brain in a jar, a pickled brain in a jar.

Assistant with my white coat and punctilious smile,
I worked it clean, scrupulous in degrees of brine.

What am I doing, doing now?
I'm singing the words to make them sweeter, faster,

wilder, neater. I out-valence your slides of singing.
Here are photos. Fold my trousers. Fold my trousers.

Folded trousers. Moulded rousers. Morose dousers.
See how I beat my spoon

so much cleaner. So much faster
I beat the radiator, they will come, they will come.

Take my fags and move the chair, I will go there.
I can sprint and run and find

only in this rush of mind
language of mine.

To rush and field and run and dance,
praise the power to insinuate.

Cheeky I am, beware!
I clutch you with words face-flung running.

Come to me, you have a care, I can see
a care of compulsion, even in shaving.

The pressure on my cheek silences
the strut of my soundings.

Come back and see me again,
come back and see me soon.

I will talk
ever so,
silently

Ever so
delicately
my mouth

stroking
words
slowly.

Happy Birth-day
Dearie Me
There's a cake with 74

My, won't everybody shout
when they see you
blow them out?

I Own Brighton Pier

Fall for me twice
memorialise me in smoke,

temper me with a smite of affection
for I own Brighton Pier.

Put all your theology in the skip
your present is not my future.

Change my bed of spilt tobacco
I make communion with your speech.

Stan the Man my sounds overlap
euphonium turns to *effigy*

and *talisman* into *tympani*
trope to a *terrible vulgarity.*

The heat draws its landscape around me
can we meet Simon John

with his sketchbooks of disaster
filed under servant and master?

Named after two saints he surely knows
where and why the wind blows?
For I own Brighton Pier.

Paint my nails black for luck
make sure my hair is greased

(please don't make me look deceased)
my waistcoat bold with stars.

Did you hear about the man who wired his house
when a light switched off another went on?

He called it *Chain of Circuitry:*
An Exploration into Modality –
A Filament Where the Heart Should Be.

It is precisely this form of immediate frivolity
we need, to conspire with authority.
For I own Brighton Pier.

There is a serious side to all this work
my nonsense is just distraction

to combat fears of frustration
as we build our institution

a runway into the sea
we will have our community.

Sue will sew the flags, John bang the drum
Harry and the lads will haul the paint.

Tamar and Gwyneth will clean the scum
so all these windows mirror light.

Our eminent Edwardians turning in their graves
think this action despicable.

But can't you see there is grace
and equanimity in being reprehensible?

Stan do you think we can make it –
with a penny arcade and a stack of manuscripts?

For I own Brighton Pier.

Take me to the Columbarium

Richmond, San Francisco

Come into the house named grief
where a man paints shadows against sun.

Meet your neighbours for an eternity party
the installation is free.

There is space near the poet
looking for the right road lost,

The Tomato Queen, The Candy Man
The Colonel and *Teller of Tall Tales.*

Here comes the father whose soldier
sleeps in a drum marked 'Do not beat'.

Here are the parents of the desert son
their tattoos marking time:

a soldier in headgear
on the bicep's bulge.

a child of four on the
mother's shoulder.

Each morning he holds her
and two sons tighter than breath.

Here is the mother on her own
trying to document with a mobile phone.

Pixels are prised to reveal
nothing but sand.

An eternity of sand with no sun
a black moon and a broken salamander
struggling on the crest of a dune.

Allow me to introduce our star
he's the pianist at the bar.

He goes to music to find
what others left behind:

I thought of you last night
(what a cue for a song)

I am Winston Churchill
you are Grace Kelly.

Like two old codgers in the park
we will always feel warmth.

I am Richard Nixon
you are Princess Diana.

Mio, Sargasso Sea
it made me so happy

because everything is what you deserve
and being guruish still

we will find hope in a situation
not of our making.

What I sing of will occur
I curate the Columbarium.

Acknowledgements

Some of these poems or earlier versions of them, have appeared in *Poetry Wales* and *Poetry Ireland*.

I am grateful to Tŷ Newydd for a bursary and *Poetry Ireland* for its 'Introductions' series, which helped this process immensely.

'The Dead Zoo, Dublin' was awarded the Ted McNulty Prize in 2008 (for best single poem published in *Poetry Ireland*).
The recognition encouraged a shy poet.

Many thanks to the alert editorial judgement and encouragement of both Amy Wack and Zoë Skoulding.

My gratitude to John a Una, Gwyneth Denver Davies, Eira Jenkins (Mrs J.), Sally Perry and Sarah MacLachlan for their support.

My special thanks to Myles Dungan and Cal for humour, data, plans and dailiness.